The Two Best Ways to Find a Job

by

J. Michael Farr
&
Susan Christophersen

from JIST the job search people

The Two Best Ways to Find a Job

© 1992 by JIST Works, Inc.

Published by JIST Works, Inc.
720 N. Park Avenue
Indianapolis, IN 46202-3490
Phone: 317-264-3720 **Fax:** 317-264-3709 **E-mail:** jistworks@aol.com
World Wide Web Address: http://www.jist.com

Other Books in the Career & Life Skills Series Include

- *An Introduction to Job Applications*
- *The Skills Advantage*
- *Why Should I Hire You?*

Cover Design by Dean Johnson Design Group
Illustration Selection and Arrangement by Mike Kreffel

Printed in the United States of America

4 5 6 7 8 9   02 01 00 99 98 97

ISBN 1-56370-040-9

Table of Contents

CHAPTER ONE—Where and How People Find Jobs...... 1

Welcome to the Job Market 1

Small Organizations Have Big Advantages 2

Where People Work 2

Additional Job Search Sources 4

Help Wanted Ads..4

Employment Agencies..5

The Government Employment Service.................................5

Private Employment Agencies...5

How Job Seekers Find Jobs: The "Hidden" Job Market 7

Why Employers Like the Hidden Job Market 7

How Employers Use the Hidden Job Market 7

Building Your Job Seeking Skills 9

CHAPTER TWO—The Two Best Job Search Techniques 11

Finding Job Leads 11

Warm Contacts: The Most Effective Job Search Method 12

Develop a Network of People You Know 12

Example: Mike Starts His Network 13

A Network Can Develop from Just One Contact 14

Who Is in a Network? 14

Example: Mike's Growing Network..................................14

Building Your Networking Skills... 16

CHAPTER THREE—Getting Ready for Your Job Search 17

Before You Start Networking 17

Know What Kind of Job You Want 18
Finding Out About Jobs That Interest You............................. 18
Know Your Skills 20
Example: Mike's Skills Statement 20
Defining Your Skills 20
JIST Cards 23
The Elements of a JIST Card 23
The Uses of a JIST Card 23
Producing Your JIST Card...23
Sample JIST Cards 24
Ways to Improve Your Job Skills.................................... 26

CHAPTER FOUR—The Network in Action.. 27

Building Your Job Search Network 27

How to Target People for Your Network 28
Create a List of Your Friends..28
More Groups of People You Know 29
Groups of People to Target for Your Network 29
Creating Other Lists 29
Network Contacts..29
Example: How Mike's Network Works for Him....................31
A Network Can Also Work for You 32
How to Get Referrals from Your Network 34
Example: How Mike Gets Referrals 35
Three Question to Ask When Getting Referrals 35
Developing Your Networking Skills 37

CHAPTER FIVE—Making Direct Contacts with Employers 39

Making "Cold" Contacts 39

Find Employers Who Need YOU 40

Using the *Yellow Pages* Index 42

Example: Maria Uses the *Yellow Pages* to Find Job Leads 44

Get Even More Leads 44

Developing Your Skills—Finding Employers to Contact 46

CHAPTER SIX—Telephone and Employer Contact Skills 47

Getting Your Foot in the Door 47

Making Telephone Contact with Employers 48

Getting to the Person Who Supervises 48

What Is a Personnel Department? 48

Why You Should Avoid the Personnel Department 48

Getting an Interview 49

Example: Maria Gathers Information for Contacting Possible Employers 49

Tips for Making Telephone Contacts 52

Keep Calling Until You Get Through 52

Calling the Person in Charge 52

Example: Maria's Practices Telephone Contacts 53

Dropping in on Employers 55

Following Up—An Important Part of Your Job Search 55

Calling Back 55

Thank-You Notes 55

Example: Maria's Thank-You Note 55

Developing Your Employer Contact Skills 57

CHAPTER ONE

Where and How People Find Jobs

The goals of this chapter are:

- ✪ *To learn where the best jobs are.*
- ✪ *To learn about traditional job search methods.*
- ✪ *To discover the "hidden" job market.*

Welcome to the Job Market

What is the job market? Is it a place where people buy and sell jobs? Well, not exactly. It would be nice if there were such a place. But the term "job market" refers to an idea, not a real place.

When you look for a job, you become part of the job market. When an employer looks for a worker to fill a job, that employer becomes part of the job market, too.

You need a job. An employer needs workers. The job market is where your needs meet. It is not an actual place, but it is very real.

The job market is not well organized. In fact, there really isn't any one place you can go to find out about job leads. In that sense it isn't like a market at all.

Finding a job can be confusing. For most people, it takes many weeks to find a job. But there are things you can do to reduce the time it takes. This book will show you how. It will also help you find the better jobs. Many people look for jobs in the wrong places. It is important to know where your best chances are.

Small Organizations Have Big Advantages

You hear a lot about big companies. They make the newspapers and the TV news. They are worth millions, or even billions, of dollars. They have thousands of people working for them.

Big companies must be where the jobs are, right? WRONG!

Most nongovernment jobs are in small companies. Small companies are often overlooked by job seekers. Yet two out of three people work in small organizations. They are also the source for over 70 percent of all new jobs.

Many large companies have actually laid off many people in the past 10 years. New and even experienced workers now find it hard to get jobs in large companies.

Small companies are also where some of the best jobs are. You can often get these jobs more easily. As you gain experience, you can often advance more rapidly.

Where People Work

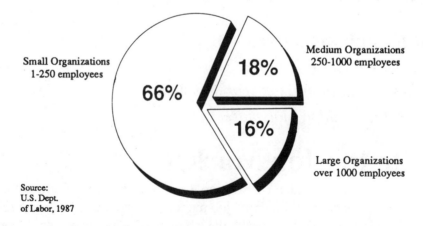

Small Organizations
1-250 employees

66%

Medium Organizations
250-1000 employees

18%

16%

Large Organizations
over 1000 employees

Source:
U.S. Dept.
of Labor, 1987

The job search methods you learn in this book will help you find jobs in smaller organizations. They will also help you find jobs in government and larger organizations, too.

✓ Checkpoint

1. What is the "job market?"

   _____

   _____

   _____

2. Where are you likely to find the best jobs?

   _____

   _____

   _____

3. What are two reasons why small companies are a good place to find jobs?

   a. _____

   _____

   _____

   b. _____

Notes

❷ Write down any questions you have or make notes about what you have just read.

   _____

   _____

   _____

   _____

   _____

   _____

   _____

   _____

   _____

Additional Job Search Sources

You need to know where to look for jobs. You also need to know HOW to look. There are many ways to find job openings. Some work better than others. In this section, we look at two sources of job leads that almost all job seekers use. These two sources are the help wanted ads and employment agencies.

Help Wanted Ads

Have you ever looked in the want ads in the newspaper? A want ad might look like this:

> **Warehouse worker:** Must have good work history. Inventory control experience helpful. Some heavy lifting is required. Full-time including some weekends and evenings. Fair pay and benefits. Call Ms. Henry, 722-7608 weekdays.

In a want ad, an employer advertises for a worker to fill a job opening. Many people think that looking in the want ads is one of the best ways to find a job. It makes sense. Right? *WRONG!*

Only about 15 percent of all job openings are advertised in the want ads. The other 85 percent are not. Most jobs are not advertised. And most job seekers read the want ads. That means that lots of people are applying for the few jobs that are advertised. Does that mean that you should not read the want ads? No. The want ads are worth reading, but you need to use other job search methods, too.

Employment Agencies

Another source of job leads are employment agencies. There are two kinds of employment agencies. One kind is run by the government. The other kind is run as a private business.

The Government Employment Service

The government employment service does not charge a fee. Some unemployed people can get unemployment pay from this office. For that reason, it is sometimes called the "unemployment office."

Employers can list their job openings at the employment service. If you qualify for the job, the employment service staff will send you to interview for those jobs.

Many employers do not list their jobs here. And only about 5 percent of all job seekers find their jobs from this source. This does not sound like much, but you should still visit your local office once a week. In some areas, as many as 30 percent of the job seekers find their jobs here. Some offices provide job-search workshops, career counseling, and other helpful services.

Ask for the same counselor each time you visit. As the counselor gets to know you, he or she will tell you about the better openings.

Private Employment Agencies

These agencies are "for-profit" businesses. They charge a fee for their services. Many agencies place want ads in the newspapers for jobs they know about. Very often, these jobs are gone by the time you answer the ad.

Only about 5 percent of all job seekers get their jobs using private agencies. Most private agencies call employers to find out about job openings. You can learn to do this yourself.

A private employment agency's fee for finding you a job may be as high as 15 percent of your yearly pay. Unless you have job skills that are very much in demand, you should not use these agencies. If you do go to them, do not sign any papers that force you to pay for jobs you find yourself.

✓ Checkpoint

1. What are some traditional job search methods? (Name ones you have learned here, as well as some that were not mentioned.)

_____

_____

_____

2. Why should you use other job search methods besides just the want ads?

_____

_____

_____

3. How are private employment agencies different from government employment agencies?

_____

_____

_____

4. How can government employment agencies help you?

_____

_____

_____

5. What are some reasons to avoid using private employment agencies?

_____

_____

_____

Notes

✪ Write down any questions you have or make notes about what you have just read.

_____

_____

_____

_____

_____

_____

_____

_____

How Job Seekers Find Jobs: The "Hidden" Job Market

Sometimes you can find good jobs in the want ads. And employment agencies know about some jobs, too. But most job openings are never advertised at all. These unadvertised jobs are hidden from most job seekers. They are part of the "hidden" job market. Most employers like to use the hidden job market. Read on to see why.

Why Employers Like the Hidden Job Market

Employers don't really like to advertise job openings. It costs money to advertise. Employers like to save money if they can.

They like to save time, too. When they place a want ad, one hundred people (or more) might answer. The employer needs to hire only one. The employer must read all the applications and then set up interviews. All this takes a lot of time.

Saving time and money are two important reasons to avoid advertising. But there is another reason that is even more important.

Job seekers who answer want ads are usually strangers. Employers—who are people just like you—feel better hiring people they know something about. They don't like to hire strangers. The next section explains how employers use the hidden job market to find workers they think they can depend on.

How Employers Use the Hidden Job Market

How does an employer find a worker to fill a job without placing an ad? Consider Frank. Frank is the manager of a grocery store called Whitman's Grocery. Frank needs to hire someone to move and unpack boxes. He needs someone who is strong and in good condition, and who can work without a lot of supervision. Most of all, Frank needs someone he can trust.

Frank does not want to have to interview a lot of people. So, he asks his other employers if they know anyone who has the skills needed for the job. Frank also talks to his friends, and other people he knows. Frank hopes that someone he knows will recommend a good worker to him.

This is how employers use the hidden job market. They depend on recommendations. The hidden job market saves employers money. It saves them time. And it often helps them avoid hiring the wrong person. This book will help you learn how to find jobs in the hidden job market.

✓ **Checkpoint**

1. What is the "hidden" job market?

   _____

   _____

   _____

   _____

2. Why do employers like to use the hidden job market?

   _____

   _____

   _____

Notes

✪ Write down any questions you have or make notes about what you have just read.

   _____

   _____

   _____

   _____

   _____

   _____

   _____

   _____

Building Your Job Seeking Skills

Gathering information is a valuable skill in your job search. Use the following activities to find out more about how people find jobs and what methods work best.

- ✪ **INDIVIDUAL ACTIVITY:** Talk to people you know (at least 10, if possible) about how they found their present or past jobs. Ask them to give you details. For example, if someone used a government employment service, ask them what they did, how long it took to find a job, what the counselor was like, and other details. If someone used a private employment agency, find out what the fees were, and if they were satisfied. Find out what percentage of the people you talked with found their current job from a want ad.

- ✪ **GROUP ACTIVITY:** Discuss the results of the above Individual Activity. Talk about different job search methods and why some work better than others.

CHAPTER TWO

The Two Best Job Search Techniques

The goals of this chapter are:

- ✪ *To learn how to get job leads from people you know.*
- ✪ *To learn how to build a job search network.*

Finding Job Leads

You now know that most jobs are not advertised. Only about 25 percent of job seekers get their jobs from help wanted ads and employment agencies. The rest of the jobs are in the "hidden" job market.

How do you find these jobs? There are two methods that most people use to find them. The first is through people they know. The second is by contacting an employer directly. We will begin learning about the first method in this chapter.

Warm Contacts: The Most Effective Job Search Method

About 40 percent of all people find their jobs through someone they know. This makes this the most effective job search method used.

Since these job leads come from our friends, relatives and other people we know, we call this approach "warm contacts." Later in this book, you will learn how to get job leads from people you do not know. We call these direct contacts "cold contacts."

Develop a Network of People You Know

When you want to find a job, you need job leads. You can find job leads by starting a job search network.

A network starts when you talk to people you know. You tell them that you are looking for a job. You talk about what kind of job you want, and what kinds of things you can do on a job. You ask people you know to give you names of people they know. You get names of people who might hire you, or who you can talk to about finding a job.

When you get the name of a person to talk to about a job, you contact that person. You call him or her on the telephone. This is a "warm contact."

Example: Mike Starts His Network

Read the story about Mike to see how he gets a job lead from a warm contact.
Mike is walking down the sidewalk. He runs into his friend Chris.

Mike: *Hey, how are you doing, Chris?*

Chris: *OK. How about you?*

Mike: *Pretty good, but I've been out of work for a while.*

Chris: *Oh, yeah? Maybe you should talk to Frank down at Whitman's Grocery. I've known Frank for years. He's the manager down there.*

Mike: *You think he might be hiring?*

Chris: *I was just talking to him about that the other day. I know he's got a job opening, and I think you've got the right skills and experience. Check it out. Tell him Chris sent you.*

By talking to Chris, Mike has started building his network. Chris will tell her other friends about Mike. In a very short time, a growing number of people will know that Mike is looking for a job.

Mike can tell other friends that he is looking for a job. If they all tell their friends, think about how many people will be contacted. A network can grow very fast.

A Network Can Develop from Just One Contact

Who Is in a Network?

There are many kinds of people besides friends who can be part of your network. Relatives, neighbors, and people you used to work with are some examples.

If you think about it, you already know many people. Read how Mike built his network of job search contacts.

Example: Mike's Growing Network

✪ Mike used to work at a shipyard. He tells people he knows there that he is looking for a job. They tell people they know.

✪ Mike plays baseball in a local league. He tells people he sees there that he is looking for a job. They tell people they know.

✪ Mike goes to church on Sundays. He tells the people he knows at his church that he is looking for a job. They tell people they know.

Here are some more people Mike includes in his network:

✪ People he knows at the hospital, where he volunteers.

✪ The parents of his friends (they tell their friends, co-workers, etc.)

✪ His own parents (they tell their friends, co-workers, etc.)

✪ People he knows in the neighborhood where he lives

✪ Like Mike, you can learn to develop your own network. The next section will show you how.

✓ **Checkpoint**

1. What is a warm contact?

   _____

   _____

   _____

2. How did Mike start building a network?

   _____

   _____

   _____

3. Why do employers like to hire people who are recommended by someone they know?

   _____

   _____

   _____

Notes

✪ Write down any questions you have or make notes about what you have just read.

_____

_____

_____

_____

_____

_____

_____

_____

_____

Building Your Networking Skills

Understanding an employer's point of view is a valuable skill for your job search. Use the activities that follow to explore why using a network is so important to both you and to employers.

✪ **INDIVIDUAL ACTIVITY:** Imagine for a moment that you are Frank, the manager at Whitman's Grocery. You (Frank) want to avoid placing an ad and taking a lot of time for interviews. You also want to hire someone you can trust. Let's say that two people came to interview for a job. One of those people is someone you don't know. The other person is Mike, a friend of Chris's. Chris sent him to you and told you that he thought that Mike would be a good worker. (You've known Chris for years.) Both Mike and the other applicant seem qualified for the job. If you were Frank, which person would you feel better about hiring? Explain why,

✪ **GROUP ACTIVITY:** Discuss the benefits for employers to find workers through people they know.

CHAPTER THREE

Getting Ready for Your Job Search

The goals of this chapter are:

- ✪ *To identify what jobs you want.*
- ✪ *To identify the skills you have for the job.*
- ✪ *To learn how to use JIST cards in your job search.*

Before You Start Networking

Your network will be one of your most important job search tools. But it's not enough to simply tell people, "I'm looking for a job." You must be clear about what type of job you want. And you must know the skills you have in order to do the job.

This chapter will help you prepare for your job search. When you do that, your network is more effective.

Know What Kind of Job You Want

Think about the type of job you want. The clearer you can be about this, the better people can help you. If you want to work in a clothing store, look for this type of job first. If you are looking for a part-time job, be flexible.

Perhaps you would be willing to work in a grocery store. Maybe you would not like to work in a restaurant. The more you can tell people about what you are looking for, the more they can help you.

✪ In the column on the left, list jobs that interest you. In the right column, list any jobs that would definitely not interest you. Use extra sheets of paper if you run out of space.

Work That I Would Like to Do	Work That I Would Not Like to Do

Now look over your list of jobs you think you would like. Ask yourself, "How much do I really know about this kind of job?" Put a check mark next to any job you listed that you need more information about. Then start looking for that information.

Finding Out About Jobs That Interest You

One way to find out about jobs is to talk to people who do them. Another way is to go to your local library. Your librarian can help you find information on careers. The books that follow are particularly helpful for most people.

✪ *Occupational Outlook Handbook*. Published by the government, this book is updated every two years. It provides descriptions of about 250 of the most popular jobs, covering 85 percent of the workforce. It is easy to read and use and provides information on wages, education and skills required, and other details. A version of this book titled *America's Top 300 Jobs* contains the same information and some libraries will allow you to borrow it.

✪ *Exploring Careers—A Young Person's Guide to Over 300 Jobs*. This is an excellent book for young people. It includes worksheets to help select careers and plan for additional training. Jobs are organized into groups, with information on over 300 jobs.

✪ *The Enhanced Guide for Occupational Exploration*. This book has descriptions for 2,500 jobs, covering over 95 percent of the workforce. The job descriptions are arranged in groups and this book is useful if you are trying to decide on a career direction.

There are many other books on careeers. A librarian can help you find them. Some libraries also have videos on different careers.

✓ Checkpoint

1. Do you have a clear idea of what jobs you really want? Explain.

   _____

   _____

   _____

2. Are there any jobs you listed that you need to find out more information about? (Think about earnings, working conditions, benefits, and other details.)

   _____

   _____

   _____

3. How can you find out more information about jobs that interest you? List some resources you have learned about. (After you list them, go out and USE them!)

   _____

   _____

   _____

Notes

✪ Write down any questions you have or make notes about what you have just read.

   _____

   _____

   _____

   _____

   _____

   _____

   _____

   _____

Know Your Skills

Your network will work better for you if you know your skills and can say clearly what they are. Think about the skills you have that would be important to an employer. You need to be able to answer the question, "Why should I hire you?"

For example, when Mike talks to all his contacts in his network, here is what he might say to them.

Mike's Skills Statement

"I am a hard worker and am willing to work weekends and vacations as well as during the week. I am also good with details and can follow instructions without being told what to do more than once. I would like to work with my hands and with people but am willing to consider other jobs."

Defining Your Skills

The activities that follow will not give you a complete picture of your skills. Everyone has hundreds of skills. But use the exercises that follow to begin to learn how to tell people what your skills are.

Good Worker Traits

List the three things about yourself that make you a good worker. Write down the most important things you can think of about yourself.

1. _____

2. _____

3. _____

Skills Inventory Checklist

✪ Place a checkmark on the line beside each skill that you believe you do well.

_____ I accept supervision	_____ I am a hard worker
_____ I get along with co-workers	_____ I am honest
_____ I have good attendance	_____ I get things done on time
_____ I am reliable	_____ I take responsibility for what I do
_____ I learn quickly	_____ I can be trusted
_____ I like to be helpful	_____ I take pride in my work

Job Skills

✪ List jobs you have done and the skills they required. Use extra pages of paper if you have had more than three jobs.

Job #1: _____

Skills

_____   _____
_____   _____
_____   _____

Job #2 _____

Skills

_____   _____
_____   _____
_____   _____

Job #3 _____

Skills

_____   _____
_____   _____
_____   _____

Equipment I Can Use

✪ List any equipment or machinery you know how to use (for example, typewriter, computer, adding machine, heavy equipment, telephone switchboard, power tools, etc.)

_____   _____
_____   _____
_____   _____

My Skills Statement

On the lines below, write a statement describing your best skills. Use the information from the activities you just completed. Pretend that someone has just asked you what sorts of things you can do on a job. Make the statement brief, highlighting your very best skills.

✪ Practice your skills statement until you sound like someone YOU would want to hire.

_____
_____
_____
_____
_____

✓ Checkpoint

1. Do you feel confident about talking about your skills? Explain.

   _____

   _____

   _____

2. What parts of your Skills Statement do you still need to work on? How can you make your statement stronger and more positive? (Think about what you are saying about yourself, and what kind of words you are using to say it.)

   _____

   _____

   _____

3. Read your Skills Statement. Do you sound like someone you would want to hire? Explain.

   _____

   _____

   _____

Notes

✪ Write down any questions you have or make notes about what you have just read.

_____

_____

_____

_____

_____

_____

_____

_____

JIST Cards

You have also practiced identifying your best skills, so that your network can work better for you. Now you will learn another important technique for making your network—and your job search— more effective.

This technique is called the JIST Card. A JIST Card is like a small resume. It is only 3 inches wide by 5 inches long, like an index card. But with this small card, you can give people a lot of information about yourself.

The Elements of a JIST Card

Here is a sample JIST Card with all its parts identified.

Sandy Zaremba   Home: (219) 232-7608
                                        Message: (219) 234-7465

Position Desired: General Office/Clerical
Skills: Over two years work experience plus one year of training in office practices. Type 55 wpm, trained in word processing operations, post general ledger, handle payables, receivables, and most accounting tasks. Responsible for daily deposits averaging $5,000 weekly. Good interpersonal skills. Can meet strict deadlines and handle pressure well.

Willing to work any hours

Organized, honest, reliable, and hard working.

The Uses of a JIST Card

During your job search, you can use your JIST Card in these ways:

- ✪ Attach one to an application when you fill one out, or attach one to your resume.
- ✪ Take it along on interviews and leave it with employers.
- ✪ Give JIST Cards to everyone in your network .
- ✪ Ask people in your netwrok to pass them on to people they know.
- ✪ Leave one with employers who won't let you fill out an application or give you an interview. (When they read your JIST Card, they might change their minds.)
- ✪ Send a JIST Card along with a thank-you note after you have an interview.

Producing Your JIST Card

If your handwriting is good, you can hand-write your JIST Cards. A better approach is to have them printed. Have yours neatly typed, making sure there are no errors. Then have several hundred printed. Most print shops will be able to do this for you at a reasonable cost.

Sample JIST Cards

John Kijek   **Home: (219) 232-9213**
                         Message: (219) 637-6643

Position Desired: Auto Mechanic

Skills: Over three years' work experience, including one year in a full-time training program. Familiar with all hand tools and basic diagnostic equipment. Can handle common repairs such as tune-ups, brakes, exhause systems, electrical and mechanical repairs. Am a fast worker, ofter completing job in less than standard time. Have all tools and can start work immediately.

Refer full-time work, any shift
Honest, reliable, good with people.
Responsible, hardworking and can solve problems.

Juanita Rodriquez   **Home: (639) 247-1643**
                        Message: (639) 361-1754
Position Desired: Warehouse Management

Skills: Six years experience plus 2 years of formal business coursework. Have supervised a staff as large as 16 people and warehousing operations covering over two acres and valued at over $14,000,000. Automated inventory operations resulting in a 30% increase in turnover and estimated annual savings over $250,000. Working knowledge of accounting, computer systems, time and motion studies, and advanced inventory. Will work any hours

Responsible, hardworking and can solve problems.
Self-motivated, dependable, learn quickly

Richard Straight Arrow   **Home: (602) 253-9678**
                  Answering Service: (602) 257-6643
Objective: Electronics installation, maintenance & sales

Skills: Four years work experience plus two year A.A. degree in Electronics Engineering Technology. Managed a 300,000/yr. business while going to school full-time, with grades in the top 25%. Familiar with all major electronics diagnostic and repair equipment. Hands-on electronics equipment and applications. Good problem solving and communications skills. Customer service oriented.

Willing to do what it takes to get the job done.

Self-motivated, dependable, learn quickly

✓ **Checkpoint**

1. How can JIST cards make your job search more effective?

   _____

   _____

   _____

2. What information should you include on your JIST Card?

   _____

   _____

   _____

3. Name some ways to use your JIST cards.

   _____

   _____

   _____

Notes

✪ Write down any questions you have or make notes about what you have just read.

   _____

   _____

   _____

   _____

   _____

   _____

   _____

   _____

Ways to Improve Your Job Skills

The Individual Activity that follows puts the information and skills you learned in this chapter into action. Read the directions for each activity thoroughly before you begin.

✪ **INDIVIDUAL ACTIVITY:** Make your own JIST Card. Rewrite it as many times as you need to, to get it just right. Get the opinion of someone you trust (such as your instructor, a former teacher of yours, a friend) about how you might make it better. Check with a local print shop for prices to have your JIST Card printed. If you type it up yourself, the printing should not be very expensive.

✪ **CLASS OR GROUP ACTIVITY:** Research jobs that interest you. You can do this by interviewing people who work in similar jobs. Another approach is to research those jobs at the library. Use the books suggested in this chapter or others the librarian suggests. Then write a report on those jobs or make a presentation to your group.

CHAPTER FOUR

The Network in Action

The goals of this chapter are:

- ✪ *To target people for your network.*
- ✪ *To see how networking brings results.*
- ✪ *To learn how to get referrals.*

Building Your Job Search Network

This chapter helps you get started on building your own job search network. It will also teach you how to get referrals from people you know. This will make your network even bigger than you may think.

How to Target People for Your Network

You probably know lots of people. Some of them you know well and some not so well. This section will help you list the people you know. There are probably more than you realize. And each one knows other people. These people can become your own job search network.

Create a List of Your Friends

Start building your network by making a list of your friends. Not just close friends. Include anyone you can think of who is friendly with you.

✪ Write their names in the left column of the form that follows. In the right column, make a note of how you will contact that person. If you always run into that person at a certain place, write that down. If you plan to call on the telephone, use that space to write in the person's telephone number.

Use an extra sheet of paper if you run out of room.

Person's Name	How I Can Make Contact

More Groups of People You Know

There are many more people besides friends to include in your network. The list that follows will give you ideas for the groups of people you know. Look it over. Put a check mark by each of the groups that makes sense for you. Then use the extra lines to add other groups that are not on the list.

You may not know some of the people in these groups very well. That doesn't matter for now.

Groups of People to Target for Your Network

_____ Relatives	_____ Members of a social club
_____ Fellow church members	_____ People who sell you things
_____ Parents of friends	_____ Former employers
_____ Neighbors	_____ People you know through sports
_____ Co-workers	_____ Guidance counselors
_____	_____
_____	_____

Creating Other Lists

Now do the same thing that you did with your list of friends. Make a separate list for each target group that you checked above. Write down the names of every person you know in each group, and how you plan to make contact. Copy as many blank forms as you need before you begin writing on the form that follows. Soon you may have dozens of people to contact. Or even hundreds. Once you begin contacting people, you can use these lists to keep track of your contacts.

✪ Put a check mark beside each name every time you talk to that person about a job lead. In the "Date Contacted" column, fill in the date you talked. This way, you can follow up on contacts you made earlier.

Network Contact Form

TARGET GROUP		
Person's Name	**How To Make Contact**	**Date Contacted**
_____	_____	_____
_____	_____	_____
_____	_____	_____
_____	_____	_____
_____	_____	_____
_____	_____	_____
_____	_____	_____
_____	_____	_____

✓ Checkpoint

1. Are you surprised by how many people you know to begin building your network? Explain.

   _____

   _____

   _____

2. Explain why it is important to keep a list of the contacts you make. Write your reasons on the lines below.

   _____

   _____

   _____

Notes

✪ Write down any questions you have or make notes about what you have just read.

   _____

   _____

   _____

   _____

   _____

   _____

   _____

   _____

Example: How Mike's Network Works for Him

     In an earlier chapter, you saw how Mike began to build his network. You should have also started thinking about who you will include in your own network.

     It might seem to you that there is a lot of talking going on in Mike's network. But you wonder, where is the action? What happens next? Read on! You'll soon find out.

     Mrs. Brown (Mike's mother) is on her coffee break at work. Sandra Parker, another employee, is at the table in the employee's lounge with her. They are talking.

Mrs. Brown:	*Did I tell you my son Mike is looking for work?*
Mrs. Parker:	*Why didn't you say so? My neighbor, Sam, mentioned just the other day that he needs a good worker down at his shop.*
Mrs. Brown:	*Do you have his telephone number?*
Mrs. Parker:	*I'll call you this evening and tell you what it is. Have Mike give Sam a call. I'll tell Sam all about him.*

That evening, Mrs. Parker gives Mike's mother the telephone number. Mike calls Sam the next morning. They schedule a meeting for later in the week. Mike has an interview!

Meanwhile, another part of Mike's network is busy, too.

Barb Riley is a friend of Mike's girlfriend. Barb works at a shipping company. She is having a meeting with her boss. Her boss, Sheila Danville, interrupts the meeting to take a telephone call.

Sheila: *(frowning) You said Jones quit? Just walked off the job? Oh, for crying out loud. Why can't we find workers we can trust? Well, ok. Do the best you can. (She hangs up the phone.)*

Barb: *Trouble, Sheila?*

Sheila: *Oh, somebody just left us in the lurch down at the loading dock. He's one of the guys I hired from that want ad we placed last month. I knew we were taking a chance with him.*

Barb: *Well, I happen to know a guy who is looking for a job right now. I've known him for a long time, Sheila, and I guarantee that he's reliable.*

Sheila: *Tell him to give me a call. Right away!*

On her lunch break, Barb calls Mike's girlfriend. Mike's girlfriend calls Mike, and gives him Sheila's telephone number. Mike calls Sheila, and they set up a meeting for the next day. Mike has another interview!

A Network Can Also Work for You

In the examples above, Mike got two job leads from people in his network. He didn't expect these job leads. He didn't find them himself. These jobs were not advertised. There was no other way he could have found out about them.

That is how the hidden job market works. The more people who are helping you look, the better. One of them will find out about a job opening. If that person is in your network, he or she will think of you. It's that simple.

✓ Checkpoint

1. How did Mike benefit from the hidden job market?

_____

_____

_____

2. Why did Sheila want to talk to Mike?

_____

_____

_____

Notes

Write down any questions you have or make notes about what you have just read.

_____

_____

_____

_____

_____

_____

_____

_____

How to Get Referrals from Your Network

You have seen three examples of how Mike's network is working:

1. *Mike talked to his friend Chris* ➡ Chris sent Mike to Frank, who manages a grocery store.

2. *Mike talked to his mother* ➡ Mike's mother talked to a co-worker, Sandra Parker ➡ Mrs. Parker knew of a job opening with her neighbor, Sam ➡ Mike called Sam.

3. *Mike's girlfriend talked to her friend, Barb Riley* ➡ Barb talked to her boss, Sheila Danville ➡ Mike called Sheila Danville.

In each of these examples, Mike got referrals. A referral is the name of someone to talk to. Chris referred Mike to Frank. Mrs. Parker referred Mike to Sam. Barb Riley referred Mike to Sheila Danville.

Every time you talk to one of your warm contacts, try to get at least TWO referrals.

Example of Getting Referrals

Mike has just finished his volunteer work at the hospital. He is in the employee locker room, gathering his things into his duffel bag before he leaves to go home. Dan Martinez, a guy Mike works with, is nearby.

Dan: *So Mike, how's the job hunt going?*

Mike: *Oh, I've been talking to a lot of people. And I've been meaning to ask you about that. Do you know anyone who has a job opening in the kind of work I do?*

Dan: *No, I don't know of a job opening. But I know someone who might have an opening later on.*

(Mike gets the person's name, company name, and telephone number from Dan.)

Mike: *This is great, Dan. Thanks. Can you think of anybody else?*

Dan: *Off the top of my head, I can think of one more person you could call. He probably doesn't have an opening but he might know someone else who does. And I'll tell you what, Mike. I'll keep thinking about it, and when I have some more names, I'll call you.*

Mike: *I really appreciate it, Dan.*

Mike got two referrals from Dan, and he might get more, too.

Three Question to Ask When Getting Referrals

When you are talking to your warm contacts about your job search, there are three questions to be sure to ask.

✪ Ask these questions one at a time. If the first question gets you a referral, write down the name and phone number. Then ask the second question. If you still haven't gotten two names, then ask the third question.

DO YOU?
1. Know of anyone who might have a job opening in my field? If no, then ....
2. Know of anyone who might know someone who has a job opening in my field? If no, then ....
3. Know someone who knows a lot of people?

Most people won't be able to give you a name for the first or even the second question. It is important to keep asking the questions until you get the referrals.

✓ Checkpoint

1. What is a referral?

_____

_____

_____

2. How are referrals important to your job search?

_____

_____

_____

3. What are the three questions to ask when you are getting referrals?

_____

_____

_____

Notes

✪ Write down any questions you have or make notes about what you have just read.

_____

_____

_____

_____

_____

_____

_____

_____

Developing Your Networking Skills

✪ **INDIVIDUAL ACTIVITY:** Call three people from the network lists you put together. Ask each of these people the three questions you learned for getting referrals. Keep notes of any information the three people give you.

✪ **CLASS OR GROUP ACTIVITY:** Have a group discussion of the results of the Individual Activity described above. Discuss how successful people were at getting referrals, how willing people were to give referrals, whether anyone got some solid job leads, and so forth.

✪ **CLASS OR GROUP ACTIVITY:** Your group is going to role-play a network. Choose one person (we'll call this person Person #1) to begin the network. Person #1 briefly tells Person #2 about the job he or she wants, and the skills he or she has. Person #2 repeats this information to Person #3, and Person #4. For example, Person #2 might say, "My friend Terry is looking for a job in retail sales. She has experience using a cash register and dealing with the public, and she has some business background." Each person passes the information on to two more people, and so on, until everyone in the group has become part of the network.

—Don't worry about memorizing the exact words Person #1 says. That's not how it works in real life, anyway. The important things to notice are:

—How clearly do Person #1's interests and skills come across?

—How quickly does the network grow when each person speaks with just two other people?

—Why is it so important for Person #1 to be very clear about what he or she wants and can do?

CHAPTER FIVE

Making Direct Contacts with Employers

The goals of this chapter are:

- ✪ *To learn how to locate employers who could use your skills.*
- ✪ *To learn good telephone skills for contacting possible employers.*
- ✪ *To learn how to make cold contacts in person.*

Making "Cold" Contacts

You have learned to find job leads from people you know. We called these warm contacts. You used warm contacts to build your network.

You will now learn about getting job leads by making cold contacts. These are contacts you make directly with an employer. You do not know these people. That is why these are called "cold" contacts.

THE TWO MOST COMMON WAYS TO MAKE COLD CONTACTS ARE:

1. Calling a company or organization on the telephone.

2. Dropping in without having an appointment.

These methods might make you feel nervous. But they work. Many people have used these methods to get interviews.

Next to warm contacts, making direct contacts with employers is the next most effective job search method. Almost 30 percent of all people get their jobs this way. This is twice as effective as answering want ads.

Find Employers Who Need YOU

Looking for a job can be lonely. When you are out of work, it seems like everyone in the world is at work but you.

You might live in a small town or a large city. Wherever you live, everywhere you go, you see people working. Everyone seems to have a place to go and something to do. Everyone, that is, but you.

The truth is, you have a place, too! Somewhere, there is a job that is right for you. Somewhere, there is an employer who needs YOU. You might find that job and that employer through your job search network.

But that is only half of your job search. The other half is to actively contact employers who may never know you exist—until you tell them!

SOMEWHERE, THERE IS AN EMPLOYER WHO NEEDS *YOU*

That is one reason that the *Yellow Pages* is a great resource for job seekers. You have an almost-complete listing of employers in your area, right at your fingertips.There is another reason the *Yellow Pages* is a good place to start. It has an index, which organizes all the businesses and services into groups, or categories. The index makes it fast and easy for you to locate the types of jobs that interest you. Get a copy of your local *Yellow Pages*. Then find the "index" section. This section is usually in the front section of the book.

Look at the sample index on page 42 of this book. Notice that some of the lines are in bold type. These are categories. The categories are listed in alphabetical order. Products and services are then listed under each category.

Using the *Yellow Pages* Index

✪ Let's look at an example. To do the following exercises, use the sample page of the index shown below.

1. Imagine that you need help filling out your tax forms. You decide to find an accountant. To do that, you go to the *Yellow Pages* Index. Find the word "Accountants" in the example below.

A

Abortion—
Alternative Organizations --------------1
Services --------------------------------------1
Abrasive Blasting Machines See
Metal Finishers' Equipment &
Supplies ----------------------------870
Sandblasting Equipment &
Supplies ----------------------------1290
Abrasives ---------------------------------------1
Absorbents ------------------------------------1
Abstracters -----------------------------------1
Access Control Systems See
Burglar Alarm Systems --------293-299
Identification Equipment &
Supplies ----------------------------746
Security Control Equipment &
Systems ----------------------------1312
Accident & Health Insurance See
Dental Service Plans------------------484
Health Maintenance
Organizations ------------------------695
Hospitalization, Medical & Surgical
Plans --------------------------------725
Insurance-------------------------------749-775
Accident Reconstruction Services --1
Accountants --------------------------------1
Accountants—
Certified Public------------------------2-5
Practitioners---------------------------6
Public----------------------------------6
**Accounting & Bookkeeping
Machines & Supplies** See
Accounts Receivable Financing See
Factors ----------------------------------590
Financing ------------------------------598,599
Acetylene—
See
Gas-Industrial & Medical-Cylinder
& Bulk --------------------------------651
Welding Equipment &
Supplies----------------------------1574
Welding See
Welding ----------------------------1572-1574
Acoustical—
Contractors-----------------------------6
Materials --------------------------------6
Partitions See
Acoustical Materials --------------6
Acrylic Displays See
Display Designers & Producers ---523
Actuaries -------------------------------6,7
**Adding & Calculating Machines &
Supplies** See
Calculating & Adding Machines &
Supplies----------------------------312

Adult—
Day Care See
Day Care Centers-Adult ----------477
Human Services
Organizations ------------------743
Social Service
Organizations----------1354,1355
Education See
Schools-Academic-Colleges &
Universities --------------1295,1296
Schools-Academic-Secondary &
Elementary ------------------1298
Advertising—
Aerial --------------------------------------8
Agencies & Counselors-------------8,9
Art & Layout Service See
Artists-Commercial ----------------68
Graphic Designers ----------------673
Calendars See
Calendars--------------------------312
Copy Writers See
Advertising Agencies &
Counselors ------------------8,9
Writers------------------------------1591
Coupons See
Advertising-Direct Mail-----------9-11
Advertising-Directory & Guide----12
Sales Promotion Service --------1288
Direct Mail------------------------------9-11
Directory & Guide----------------------12
Displays See
Display Designers &
Producers ---------------------523
Display Fixtures & Materials ----523
Signs ------------------------------1342-1350
Distributing Service See
Distributing Service-Circular,
Sample, Etc.--------------------523
Matches See
Matches----------------------------860
Newspaper -----------------------------12
Novelties See
Advertising Specialties---------13,14
Novelties-Retail---------------------935
Novelties-Whsle & Mfrs ---------935
Outdoor ----------------------------------12
Periodical---------------------------------12
Photographers See
Photographers-
Commercial ------------1027,1028
Research See
Market Research & Analysis----854
Telemarketing Services --------1406
Searchlights -----------------------------13
Specialties----------------------------13,14
Television -------------------------------14
Transit & Transportation --------------14
Typographers See
Typographers----------------------1512
Aerial—
Advertising See
Advertising-Aerial -------------------8
Lift Equipment See
Cranes--------------------------------469

Aikido Instruction See
Karate & Other Martial Arts
Instruction --------------------789-792
Air—
Ambulance Service See
Aircraft Charter, Rental & Leasing
Service ----------------------26-28
Ambulance Service-Emergency &
Medical------------------------38,39
Balancing --------------------------------15
Brakes See
Brake Service --------------------277-283
Cargo & Package Express
Service --------------------------------15
Charter Service See
Aircraft Charter, Rental & Leasing
Service ----------------------26-28
Travel Agencies &
Bureaus --------------1472-1478
Cleaning & Purifying Equipment-----15
Compressors See
Compressors-Air & Gas-----------402
Compressors-Air & Gas-
Renting------------------------------402
Conditioning Contractors &
Systems ----------------------------16-25
Conditioning Equipment-Room
Units ------------------------------------26
Conditioning Equipment & Service-
Automobile See
Automobile Air Conditioning
Equipment-Sales &
Service ----------------123-125
Automobile Repairing &
Service --------------------194-207
Conditioning Equipment & Systems-
Repairing------------------------------26
Conditioning Supplies & Parts -------26
Courier Service ------------------------26
Craft Dealers See
Aircraft Dealers ----------------------29
Craft Leasing & Rental Service See
Aircraft Charter, Rental & Leasing
Service ----------------------26-28
Craft Parts See
Aircraft Equipment, Parts &
Supplies ----------------------------29
Curtains & Screens-------------------26
Cylinders See
Cylinders-Air & Hydraulic--------471
Valves --------------------------------1522
Duct Cleaning See
Ventilating Systems-Cleaning-1526
Express Service See
Air Cargo & Package Express
Service --------------------------------15
Air Courier Service------------------26
Filters See
Filters-Air & Gas --------------------597
Freight Service See
Air Cargo & Package Express
Service--------------------------------15
Hoists See
Hoists --------------------------------716
Line Companies See

Air—(Cont'd)
Pumps-Dealers------------1185-1188
Valves --------------------------------1522
Purifying Equipment See
Air Cleaning & Purifying
Equipment----------------------------15
Taxi Service See
Aircraft Charter, Rental & Leasing
Service ----------------------26-28
Airport Transportation Service ---32
Tools See
Tools-Pneumatic ----------------1451
Aircraft—
Brokers--------------------------------26
Charter, Rental & Leasing
Service --------------------------26-28
Dealers----------------------------------29
Equipment, Parts & Supplies---------29
Hangars See
Airports --------------------------32,33
Insurance See
Insurance --------------------749-775
Mfrs --------------------------------------29
Schools----------------------------------29
Servicing & Maintenance-------------29
Upholsterers------------------------------29
Airline—
Companies-----------------------29-32
Ticket Agencies ------------------------32
Airplane Model Supplies See
Hobby & Model Construction
Supplies-Retail----------------714-716
Airplanes See
Aircraft Dealers ------------------------29
Airport—
Equipment & Supplies ----------------32
Transportation Service ----------------32
Airports---------------------------------32,33
Alarm Systems See
Automobile Alarm Systems --------125
Burglar Alarm Systems --------293-299
Fire Alarm Systems-----------------599
Medical Alarms----------------------866
Security Control Equipment &
Systems ----------------------------1312
Smoke Detectors & Alarms --------1352
Albums-------------------------------------33
**Alcoholism Information & Treatment
Centers** ------------------------------33-37
Alignment Service-Automotive See
Automobile Repairing &
Service ----------------------------194-207
Wheel Alignment, Frame & Axle
Servicing-Automotive ----1575,1576
Alloys--------------------------------------37
Alteration Contractors See
Building Contractors ----------289,290
Carpenters--------------------------317
Contractors-Alteration----------439-447
Contractors-General ----------450-453
Home Improvements------------720-722
Alterations-Clothing----------------37,38
**Alternators & Generators-
Automotive** See
Aluminum-----------------------------38

2. "Accountants" is in bold type. It is the name of a category. Under "Accountants" there is a list of words in lighter type. On the lines below, write these words and the numbers that appear next to them.

_____

_____

_____

_____

_____

3. The words you just wrote are types of accounting services. The numbers next to them are the page numbers where you will find each kind of accountant.

   If you were using the actual *Yellow Pages* that had this index, you would turn to pages 2-5 to find "Certified Public Accountants." On those pages, you would find addresses and telephone numbers of the businesses that provide this service.

✪ Now try locating something in your own *Yellow Pages*.

4. Perhaps you are thinking about going to school. You want to find information about vocational education. Follow the steps below to find that information.

✪ Find "Vocational" in the index. (Remember, it is organized in alphabetical order.) In many cases, you may have to look up several categories to find what you want. In this example, you could also look under the category "Schools."

5. On the lines below, list all the headings in regular type under the word "Vocational." Also list the page numbers that appear next to them.

____

____

____

____

____

6. Look at the first heading you listed above. In your *Yellow Pages* directory, turn to the page number you wrote down.

7. Write the names, addresses, and telephone numbers of three of the services you find.

____

____

____

____

____

____

____

____

____

4 Accountants TELL THE ADVERTISER—"I FOUND YO

A

Accountants-Certified Public (Cont'd)

B

FARRIS JACQUELINE A
6008 N Keystone Av ------------------257-3225

C

FAUROTE DENNIS L CPA

HAINES RENITA CPA
8328 Masters Rd ---------------------849-6385
HAIR & COMPANY CPA
5257 N Tacoma Av Suite 8 -----------255-2730
HALL COOK & COMPANY PC
8888 Keystone Crsg Suite 710 Indpls -843-2699
HALL GARY L CPA
8888 Keystone Crsg Suite 710 Indpls -843-2699

JANUARY & ENGEL 688 E 63 --------
JENKINS DOUGLAS CPA
8555 River Rd Suite 360 Indpls -----
JERMAN GALLAGHER & SHERCK
350 E New York Suite 220 ---------
JOHNSON TERRY L CPA
350 E New York Suite 220 --------
JOHNSTON SHAUB & CO CPA'S I

Example: Maria Uses the *Yellow Pages* to Find Job Leads

Read the story that follows to see how Maria Cortez used the *Yellow Pages* to find job leads.

Maria is looking for a job. She once worked on a construction crew. She learned how to work certain kinds of equipment. Maria liked the job. She would like to find another one like it.

Maria turned to the Yellow Pages index. She looked under "C" for Construction.

Using a pencil, Maria put a check mark beside the headings that interested her. Then she wrote down the page numbers of each of those headings. She wrote them in a notebook that she had labeled "Job Prospects."

Maria turned to the page which listed "Building Contractors." In her "Job Prospects" notebook, she wrote the names and telephone numbers of all the companies she wanted to contact about jobs she could do.

Maria did this for each of the headings she had checked off in the index. Soon she had a long list of companies to call.

Get Even More Leads

Maria looked under "Construction" since she was interested in these jobs. And she found some good leads. But here is a way you can find many more job leads.

Look at every listing in the index. As you do, ask yourself, "Would this type of organization be able to use a person with my skills?" If the answer is "yes," then mark that listing. Use the system that follows:

- ✪ Write "1" if that organization sounds interesting to you.
- ✪ Write "2" if you are not sure.
- ✪ Write "3" if that organization does not sound interesting to you.

If Maria did this, one of the many listings she would find would be "Hospitals." This type of organization could use her skills. So she would then mark that listing. Let's say that she marked it with a "1" because it sounded interesting. Later, she could contact the hospitals and try to get a job using her construction and building repair skills there. In the next chapter, you will see how Maria learned to make telephone calls to these employers.

✓ Checkpoint

1. Describe how the *Yellow Pages* index is organized.

   _____

   _____

   _____

2. What are two reasons why the *Yellow Pages* are an excellent resource for finding job leads?

   _____

   _____

   _____

Notes

❂ Write down any questions you have or make notes about what you have just read.

   _____

   _____

   _____

   _____

   _____

   _____

   _____

   _____

Developing Your Skills—Finding Employers to Contact

✪ **INDIVIDUAL ACTIVITY:** Begin your job prospects notebook, like Maria's. Continue using the *Yellow Pages* index to locate possible employers. Then put the names, addresses, and telephone numbers in your notebook. Keep track of who you contact, and when.

✪ **GROUP ACTIVITY:** Try to think of any other resources you might use besides the *Yellow Pages* to provide possible job leads. Assign group members to research the ideas your group comes up with. For example, your community may offer directories of local agencies or services.

CHAPTER SIX

Telephone and Employer Contact Skills

The goals of this chapter are:
- ✪ *To learn good telephone skills for making cold contacts effectively.*
- ✪ *To learn other contact skills that you will use in your job search.*

Getting Your Foot in the Door

To get a job, you need to be able to communicate. You need to let people know who you are and what you can do.

And, of course, you need to get interviews with people who can hire you. To get interviews, you need to know how to get your foot in the door at organizations that might be able to use your skills.

Read on to learn more ways to make your contact with possible employers successful.

Making Telephone Contact with Employers

When you are ready to call a possible employer, there are two goals to keep in mind:

1. Get to the person who supervises people with your skills.
2. Get an interview.

Getting to the Person Who Supervises

When you are contacting an employer for the first time, you will need to get the name of a person to talk to about a job in your field, the best time to call that person, and person's job title (for example, Supervisor, Foreman, Manager).

This sounds fairly simple, and often, it is. But it can sometimes present a problem. That's because job seekers might be sent to the company's personnel department.

What Is a Personnel Department?

One of the main jobs of a personnel department is to find good employees. There is, however, another critical job for the personnel department. It is to screen out job applicants. If your application does not look just right, your application will often be rejected.

Why You Should Avoid the Personnel Department

About two out of three people now work in small organizations (250 or fewer). Most of them are not large enough to have a separate personnel department. Even many big organizations don't have them. You want to get to the person who will supervise you. They are the ones who will make a decision to hire you. That is why getting to them is your first goal in contacting an employer.

The sample telephone script that appears later will help you avoid being steered to the personnel department.

Getting an Interview

Your other goal in contacting an employer is to get an interview. An interview is a meeting you have with an employer to discuss what the job is and why you are qualified to do it.

Earlier, you saw how Maria Cortez made a list of employers to call from the *Yellow Pages*. Now you can read about how she accomplishes the two goals of making contact on the telephone.

Example: Maria Gathers Information for Contacting Possible Employers

Maria looks at the list she made of job prospects. She dials the number of the first company on her list. The telephone is answered by a receptionist.

Receptionist: *A and B Builders... may I help you?*

Maria: *Hi. I'm looking for a job and I'd like to talk to someone about that.*

Receptionist: *I'll direct your call to personnel. Hold, please, while I transfer you.*

The person Maria talks to in personnel tells her to come in and fill out an application. Did Maria get to the person who could supervise her? No. What could she have done differently? Maria tries again, this time with the second company on her list.

Receptionist: *Good morning. This is Jones Contracting. May I help you?*

Maria: *Hi. Could I speak with the person who supervises your building crews?*

Receptionist: *What is the nature of your call, please?*

Maria: *I am looking for a job.*

Receptionist: *I'll transfer your call to personnel.*

Whoops! It happened again. How can Maria get the name of someone to talk to outside of the personnel department? She tries again.

Maria:	*Hello. My name is Maria Cortez. I'd like the name of the person who supervises the construction crews.*
Receptionist:	*What is the nature of your call?*
Maria:	*I have some information to send this person, and I'd like to get the correct spelling of the name and the address.*
Receptionist:	*His name is John O'Keefe. The address is 9101 Market Street, zip code 44502.*
Maria:	*Mr. O'Keefe's telephone number would be helpful, too.*
Receptionist:	*His extension is 381.*
Maria:	*If I should need to contact him by telephone, when is the best time to reach him?*
Receptionist:	*He is usually in the office in the mornings between 8 and 10. After that he is in and out a lot.*
Maria:	*Thanks very much. I appreciate your help.*

This time, Maria got the information she needed. What did she do that was different from the first two calls she made? The next exercise will help you answer that question.

✓ Checkpoint

✪ Fill in the blanks and answer the questions that follow.

1. Maria asked for the _____ *(job title)* of a group of workers.

2. Before making the call, Maria decided to ask for a specific area of the company, which was
_____ *(the type of work done by those workers).*

3. When the receptionist asked Maria why she was calling, Maria did not say she was looking for a job. Instead, she said she needed the supervisor's name so she could...

_____

_____

_____

4. After she got the supervisor's name and address, what else did Maria ask for?

_____

_____

_____

5. What other information did Maria get that would help her contact Mr. O'Keefe?

_____

_____

_____

6. At the end of their conversation, Maria remembered to _____ the receptionist for the information.

Notes

✪ Write down any questions you have or make notes about what you have just read.

_____

_____

_____

_____

_____

_____

_____

_____

Tips for Making Telephone Contacts

✪ Be courteous.

✪ Give your name, sound professional.

✪ Get the name of someone in charge. (Not someone in the personnel department.)

✪ Find a way to state your business without saying you are looking for a job (For example, "I have some business to discuss," "I have some information I believe will interest him or her."

✪ Get the person's telephone number, business address, or both.

✪ Thank the receptionist—you may be speaking with that person again!

Keep Calling Until You Get Through

You might not always get through to the person you want to reach. There will be times when the best you will get is a transfer to the personnel department. Or the receptionist might refuse to give you the name of someone unless you state exactly why you are calling.

But most of the time, you will find people who are willing to help you. So keep trying, and don't be discouraged by the ones who screen you out.

Calling the Person in Charge

Maria used the *Yellow Pages* to find employers. She made calls to find the names of people to contact. Now she is ready to call Mr. O'Keefe.

Maria is very nervous. She does not like calling people she does not know. She is afraid she will say the wrong thing, or sound as nervous as she feels.

Tom Duncan, Maria's friend, has recently been through the job search process himself. He knows how Maria feels.

Tom suggests to Maria that they practice calling an employer together. He will pose as an employer. Maria can then rehearse what she is going to say.

Example: Maria Practices Telephone Contacts

Maria pretends to call Mr. O'Keefe on the telephone. Tom poses as Mr. O'Keefe, answering the telephone.

Maria: *May I speak with Mr. O'Keefe, please?*

Tom: *This is Mr. O'Keefe.*

Maria: *Hello. My name is Maria Cortez. I am interested in a position on one of your construction crews, and I would like to meet with you to tell you about my skills and experience.*

Tom: *Well, go ahead and send me your resume and I'll take a look at it.*

Maria: *I'd be happy to send you my resume, but I'd really like to set up an appointment with you at your convenience.*

Tom: *I don't have any actual job openings right now, Ms. Cortez.*

Maria: *I see. I know you must be very busy, but I'd like to bring my resume to you in person and spend a few minutes talking with you. That way, if you should need a person with my skills later on, you'll already know something about me.*

Tom: *That sounds like a good idea. Can you come to my office Wednesday at 9 a.m.?*

Maria: *That sounds fine. Thank you very much.*

Maria continued to practice until she felt confident enough to make the real call to Mr. O'Keefe. When she did, she got an interview.

✓ Checkpoint

1. What are the two goals to keep in mind when you make contact with a possible employer?

   _____

   _____

   _____

2. Why is it best to avoid the personnel department? (Who should you try to contact instead?)

   _____

   _____

   _____

Notes

✪ Write down any questions you have or make notes about what you have just read.

_____

_____

_____

_____

_____

_____

_____

_____

_____

Dropping in on Employers

You have learned skills to locate employers who might hire you and to make contact with them. You can use these same skills in an even more direct way than calling on the telephone. Stopping by a place of business or an organization without an appointment is OK.

Some employers will be willing to see you on short notice. For those who can't see you, the visit can still be worthwhile. You can ask to make an appointment for another day. You can also leave your JIST card and resume with the receptionist, and ask that they be passed on to the appropriate person. While you're there, you can gather information about the organization and the job.

Following Up—An Important Part of Your Job Search

The term "follow-up" refers to things you should do after you make contact with anyone in your job search network—especially employers. Follow up with a call back later and send a thank-you note.

Calling Back

In an earlier chapter, you learned that it is important to keep track of who you make contact with in your job search network, and when you make contact. This is so that you can make follow up contacts later. People might have more information for you than they had when you first talked.

It is especially important to call back an employer after you make contact—for instance, if you have an interview. Call a few days or a week later, to let the employer know you are still interested in the job.

Thank-You Notes

Everyone likes to be recognized for being helpful. But a thank-you note is more than a nice gesture—it's an excellent job search tool. Write thank-you notes to anyone who helps you in your job search. Send notes to employers immediately after an interview. So few job seekers do this, that you will make a very good impression. And the employer is likely to remember you when it comes time to make a decision about who to hire.

Here is an example of a thank-you note. Maria sent this to Mr. O'Keefe a day after they met for an interview.

Example: Maria's Thank-You Note

Maria wrote this inside a simple, light-colored card which she bought at a stationery shop.

July 4, 19XX

Dear Mr. O'Keefe,

I want to thank you for taking the time to meet with me recently. I was very impressed with your company and the state-of-the-art equipment your crews use. I am interested in this kind of work and would be willing to work hard if you have a job opening in the future. I look forward to meeting with you again.

Sincerely,

Maria Cortez

Maria Cortez

✓ Checkpoint

1. Why is "dropping in" on a possible employer worthwhile?

   _____

   _____

   _____

2. What does it mean to "follow up?"

   _____

   _____

   _____

Notes

✪ Write down any questions you have or make notes about what you have just read.

   _____

   _____

   _____

   _____

   _____

   _____

   _____

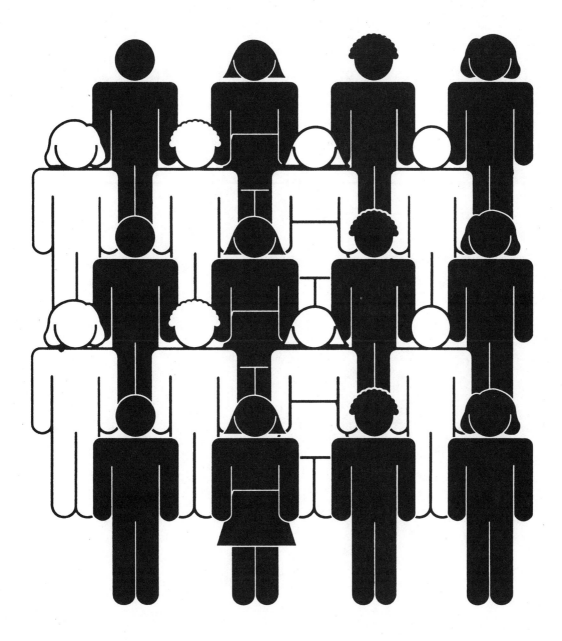

Developing Your Employer Contact Skills

Practicing skills helps you build confidence. The activities that follow can help you make your contacts with possible employers more effective.

✪ **INDIVIDUAL ACTIVITY:** Write a telephone script to use as practice for making telephone calls to possible employers. Keep it short and write the way you talk. Your script should include your name, why you are calling, and a statement about your skills and what makes you a good worker. You can use your JIST Card as the basis for a phone script. Your script should end with the question, "When may I come in for an interview?"

✪ **GROUP ACTIVITY:** Break into groups of two's and practice the telephone scripts you wrote. One person will be the job seeker and the other will be the employer. Remember the two goals: 1) Get to the person who supervises; and 2) Get an interview.

Notes